Maurice
RAVEL

PAVANE
pour une Infante défunte
Orchestra version

Edited by
Carl Simpson

Study Score
Partitur

SERENISSIMA MUSIC, INC.

PREFACE

In July of 1895, after having failed to win the harmony or piano prizes, the twenty-year-old Maurice Ravel dropped out of the Paris Conservatoire. Before resuming his studies – in Gabriel Fauré's composition class in January 1898 – Ravel apparently decided to devote himself to composing. The two and one-half year respite saw the creation of several works: *Un Grand Sommeil noir* (August 1895), *Menuet antique* (November 1895 – Ravel's first published work), *Sites auriculaires* (November 1895 - December 1897), *Sainte* (December 1896), and an early one-movement *Sonate pour piano et violon* (April 1897).

In the months after joining Fauré's class, Ravel was one of the students invited to attend some of the more renowned Parisian musical *soirées*, including those hosted by Mme. René de Saint-Marceaux and Mme. Princesse Edmond de Polignac, who commissioned the original piano version of the present work in 1899. The *Pavane pour une Infante défunte* was published the following year by the Paris firm E. Demets, but had to wait until April 5, 1902 for its concert premiere by Ravel's classmate and good friend, the pianist Ricardo Viñes. Much to its composer's surprise, the *Pavane* became immensely popular – so much so that an American edition (by Rudolph Ganz) appeared by 1906. Ravel later criticized it for being "poor in form" and displaying "excessive influence of Chabrier."

Even so, Ravel thought enough of the work that he prepared the exquisite setting "pour petit orchestre" in the latter part of 1910. Through his use of orchestral forces common in classical period of Mozart and Haydn, including two natural horns in G (valveless instruments that were obsolete by 1910), the composer evokes a past epoch. This strain of "archaic lyricism" that can be traced in his work from the *Menuet antique* all the way up through the "Adagio" for the *Concerto pour piano et orchestre* of 1931. The orchestral version received its premiere in England on February 27, 1911 at the Manchester Gentlemen's Concerts under the baton of Henry Wood. The *Pavane* was first recorded (on disk) in its orchestral setting in 1921 by Francis Touche conducting the Orchestre des Concerts Touche. (Grammophone-France, 78 rpm, 30 cm, acoustic. W356, L548.)

The present edition is based upon the following sources:

I. The full score published by E. Demets in 1910, plate number E. 1542 D., 7 pages. Demets was acquired by the publisher Max Eschig in 1924 or 1925. Thus there are several later printings bearing the name of the successor firm. In addition, this score has been reprinted in the United States over the years by Luck's Music, Inc. and Dover Publications, among others.

II. The original piano version, which was first issued in 1900 by E. Demets, plate number E. 623 D., 5 pages. In addition to numerous printings over the years by the successor Max Eschig, the work has been reprinted extensively in the United States and elsewhere, most recently in a collection of Ravel's piano works issued by Dover.

The primary source of the present edition is the Demets full score, which shows some evidence of having been carefully proofed by the composer in light of the small number of errors. The Demets score's (and subsequent reprints') main weakness lies in its somewhat crowded layout which can result in overlooking some of Ravel's numerous meticulously placed articluation markings. The composer also changed a number of tempo and expressive indications from those that appeared in the piano score published a decade earlier. In the present edition, the tempi from the piano version have been placed in footnotes or bracketed. The fermata at measure 27 appears in the piano version only and has thus been placed in parentheses. The few editorial dynamics added have likewise been enclosed in brackets. Both score and parts for this edition have been newly engraved, with a much more spacious layout designed to facilitate performance.

Carl Simpson
Summer, 2004

Pavane pour une Infante défunte
(1899 - Orchestrated 1910)

MAURICE RAVEL
edited by Carl Simpson

* Piano version: **Azzez doux, mais d'une sonorité large**

* Piano version: **Tres lontain**

8

* Piano version: *un peu plus lent*

** Piano version: **Reprenez le mouvement**

*Piano version: **En mesure**

* Piano version additionally states: *subitement très douz et très lié*

17

* Piano version: **Reprenez le mouvement**

www.ingramcontent.com/pod-product-compliance
Lightning Source LLC
Chambersburg PA
CBHW081026040426
42444CB00014B/3374